Today Is Monday in New York

Traditional Song Adapted by Johnette Downing
Illustrated by Deborah Ousley Kadair

Wiggle Worm Publishing

New Orleans 2024

Today Is Monday in New York

Published by Wiggle Worm Publishing, PO Box 13367, New Orleans, LA 70185
All rights reserved

To all the New Yorkers in my life who helped me with this book. A special thanks
to Michael, Nancy, Norman, Jeri, Stanford, and Nathan's Famous Hot Dogs. — J.D.

In memory of Morry Larrea, awesome uncle, caring brother-in-law, special friend.
— D.O.K.

Today Is Monday.

Today is Monday.
Monday **apples**.

All you lucky children
come and eat it up.
Come and eat it up!

Today Is Tuesday.

Today is Tuesday.
Tuesday **pastrami**,
Monday apples.

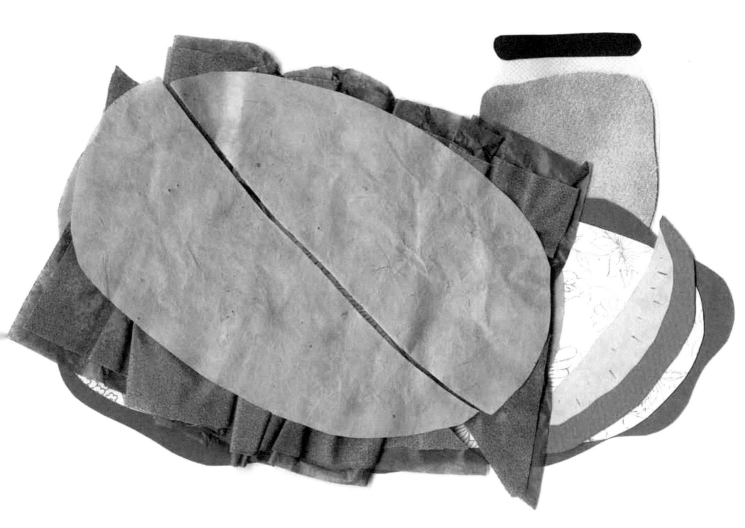

All you lucky children
come and eat it up.
Come and eat it up!

Today Is Wednesday.

Today is Wednesday.
Wednesday **Buffalo wings**,
Tuesday pastrami,
Monday apples.

All you lucky children
come and eat it up.
Come and eat it up!

Today Is Thursday.

Today is Thursday.
Thursday **Nathan's hot dogs**,
Wednesday Buffalo wings,
Tuesday pastrami,
Monday apples.

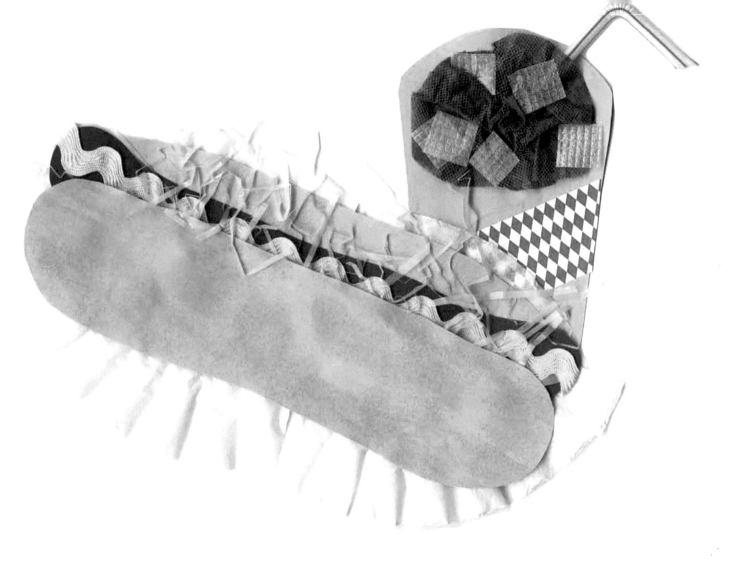

All you lucky children
come and eat it up.
Come and eat it up!

Today Is Friday.

Today is Friday.
Friday **cheesecake**,
Thursday Nathan's hot dogs,
Wednesday Buffalo wings,
Tuesday pastrami,
Monday apples.

All you lucky children
come and eat it up.
Come and eat it up!

Today Is Saturday.

Today is Saturday.
Saturday pizza,
Friday cheesecake,
Thursday Nathan's hot dogs,
Wednesday Buffalo wings,
Tuesday pastrami,
Monday apples.

All you lucky children
come and eat it up.
Come and eat it up!

Today Is Sunday.

Today is Sunday.
Sunday **bagels and lox**,
Saturday pizza,
Friday cheesecake,
Thursday Nathan's hot dogs,
Wednesday Buffalo wings,
Tuesday pastrami,
Monday apples.

All you lucky children
come and eat it up.
Come and eat it up.
Come and eat it up!

Word Menu

Apples

In 1976, the apple was adopted as the state fruit of New York. Popular varieties include Mcintosh, Golden Delicious, Winesap, Empire, Red Delicious, Cortland, Rome, Crispin, Gala, and Fuji.

Bagels and lox

(BAY-gulz) Bagels are chewy, doughnut-shaped bread rolls boiled in water and then baked in an oven until the crust is brown. In New York, bagels are eaten with cream cheese and lox (cured salmon) and are traditionally served on Sundays, though they can be enjoyed any day of the week. When in New York City, ask for "bagels with a schmear," which means bagels with a generous helping of cream cheese.

Buffalo wings

Buffalo chicken wings were created on October 30, 1964, by Teressa Bellissimo at Frank & Teressa's Anchor Bar in Buffalo, New York to feed her son's hungry friends. Buffalo wings are deep-fried chicken wings served with a hot sauce, celery stalks, and blue cheese dressing.

Nathan's hot dogs

In 1916, a Polish immigrant named Nathan Handwerker opened a small hot dog stand in Coney Island, New York. Based on a recipe developed by his wife, Ida, Nathan's Famous are regarded as being among the best hot dogs in the world. "Hot dogs from the cart" are also a favorite throughout the city, served by sidewalk vendors with mustard and sauerkraut.

New York cheesecake

Cheesecake dates back to the first century A.D. in Rome. However, New Yorkers will tell you that you haven't eaten cheesecake until you've eaten New York cheesecake! Famous in delicatessens and restaurants since the 1920s, the silky, smooth, rich New York cheesecake is made with pure cream cheese, cream, eggs, and sugar.

New York pizza

In 1905, Gennaro Lombardi opened the first pizzeria in the United States at 53 Spring Street in New York City. Similar to the Naples, Italy variety, traditional New York-style pizza is hand-tossed with a thin, wide crust topped with light tomato sauce and mozzarella cheese. "Pizza by the slice" is a large slice that is often eaten folded in half. New Yorkers will tell you that it is the New York tap water that gives the dough its unique texture. Thick, square pizza slices called "Sicilian" are also popular.

Pastrami on rye

Brought to the United States by Jewish immigrants, pastrami on rye with spicy mustard is a classic New York deli sandwich. Pastrami is made from beef brisket that is cured in brine, coated with spices, and smoked. It is then sliced medium width and piled high between two pieces of hot rye bread. This sandwich is often served with coleslaw or a Kosher dill pickle.

Official State Foods of New York

State fruit—apple (1976)
State beverage—milk (1981)
State muffin—apple muffin (1987)
State freshwater fish—brook trout (1975)
State marine or saltwater fish—striped bass (2006)
State shell—bay scallops (1988)
State tree—sugar maple (1956)

Other foods associated with New York are egg creams (a drink made with milk, seltzer, and chocolate syrup), Manhattan clam chowder, corned beef on rye, beef on weck (roast beef on a kummelweck roll), New York strip steak, Long Island duckling, black and white cookies, Jell-O, potato chips, Thousand Island dressing, Waldorf salad, maple syrup, garbage plate (a dish that pairs a meat with a side dish, such as a hamburger with fries or macaroni), Brooklyn bialy (a small seasoned roll), spiedies (marinated cubes of meat cooked on a skewer), knishes (fried or baked dough with potato, spinach, mushroom, kasha, or meat filling), cheddar, potatoes, salt potatoes (new white potatoes boiled in salted water), cabbage, and corn.

Today Is Monday in New York

Traditional song with adapted lyrics by Johnette Downing
© 2010 Johnette Downing, Wiggle Worm Records

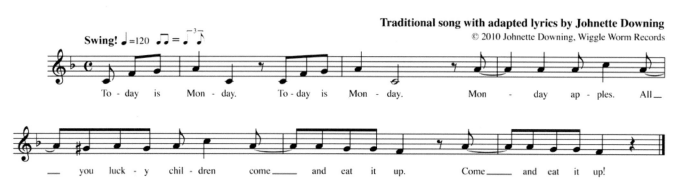

Swing! ♩=120

To - day is Mon - day. To - day is Mon - day. Mon - day ap - ples. All __

__ you luck - y chil - dren come ___ and eat it up. Come ___ and eat it up!

Printed in France by Amazon
Brétigny-sur-Orge, FR

20341037R00020